# food style

# seafood

## acknowledgements

Firstly, I would like to express my deepest thanks to Anne Wilson and Catie Ziller for the opportunity to write three more books and for having the clear publishing vision that I have been privileged to be a part of for the past four years. To Susan Gray, my patient and careful editor, for picking up all the "oopses". To Marylouise Brammer, the talented designer who has given time, love and dedication to making these books truly beautiful. To Ben Dearnley, the photographer, and Kristen Anderson, the food stylist, for blessing me with their professionalism, friendship but most of all talent for a very special six weeks—thank you for your generosity. To Anna Waddington, project manager and walking angel, for organizing me and my manicness. To Jane Lawson, the new torchbearer, for listening, laughing and yumming with me. To David, Bec, Kate, Lulu and Melita for sharing my passion for food and for making work a special place. To Valli Little and Angela Tregonning for testing and tasting my recipes with me and sharing their knowledge. To Donna Hay, lady princess, gifted fellow foodie and friend, just for being who she is. To Mum, Matt, Relle, Rhearn, Nathan, Trace, Scottie, Paulie and Kim for their positive feedback, love and patience. To Penel, Michael, Shem and Gabe for a bond and sealant in the form of love that keeps me afloat. To Jude, for doing the yards with me with such honesty and caring. To Dundee for the pearls of wisdom. To Mel, Chaska, Rod, Pete, Fish, Olivia, Annie, Daz, Col, Richie, Melanie, Sean, Anne, George, Yvette, Woody, Ulla, Glenn, Boyd, Sal, Birdie and Dave for enjoying eating as much as I enjoy cooking. Thanks too to Con at Demcos for providing the stunningly delicious seafood for this book. A huge hug and truckloads of thanks to Dun, Richie and Col for allowing us to invade their home for two weeks of shooting.

Finally, I would like to dedicate this book to my baby sister Paulie, who loves to fish with me in blind faith that one day we shall be blessed with a catch worthy of eating.

The publisher wishes to thank the following for their generosity in supplying props for the book: Accoutrement; Bison Homewares; Boda Nova; The Bay Tree; Country Road Homewear; David Jones; Domestic Pots—pieces by Lex Dickson, Phil Elson, Simon Reece, Victor Greenaway, Helen Stephens; Culti; Empire Homeware; Ikea; Papaya Studio; Wild Rhino.

Front cover: lobster kiev, page 66.

food style

seafood

jody vassallo

TIME
LIFE
BOOKS

# contents

Enhance fresh seafood with marinades and bastes inspired by cuisines from around the world.

sesame oil, lemon juice, kecap manis, ginger, toasted sesame seeds—use for fish, shrimp, octopus, mussels or oysters

olive tapenade and extra-virgin olive oil, applied with a rosemary sprig—use for tuna, swordfish or salmon

tandoori paste, plain yogurt and chopped fresh mint—use for shrimp, fish, scallops or scampi

crushed mixed peppercorns, shredded preserved lemon, garlic and olive oil—use for fish, shrimp or lobster

green peppercorns, hazelnut oil, orange zest and juice with fennel brush—use for squid, shrimp, fish or scallops

whole grain mustard, balsamic vinegar, honey, chives and olive oil—use for squid, shrimp, mussels, fish or scallops

bottled chili paste, basil leaves, brown sugar and sesame oil—use for scallops, shrimp, octopus, squid or fish

bottled asian satay sauce, coconut cream, lime juice and cilantro—use for scallops, fish or shrimp

Thread seafood onto natural skewers for extra flavor when barbecued. Try …

peeled shrimp and kaffir lime or young lime leaves on stalks of lemongrass

strips of fresh tuna woven with lemon slices onto baby branches of bay leaf

cleaned baby squid threaded onto fresh fennel stalks

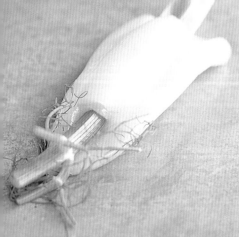

succulent scallops spiked onto slim young bamboo stalks

cubes of succulent fresh salmon
spiked onto fresh kaffir lime branches

firm white fish fillets between halved red
chiles, pierced onto basil sprigs

a shrimp, a bay leaf and your favorite fish
skewered onto thin sugar cane stalks

blocks of swordfish and slices of lemon
pierced with sprigs of fragrant rosemary

Salmon roe—those bright orange
bubbles that burst in your mouth—
are the eggs of the female fish.

## bruschetta with salmon tartare and roe bubbles

1 italian wood-fired loaf bread, cut
into 1/2-inch thick slices
3 cloves garlic, cut in half
extra-virgin olive oil
1 lb salmon fillets, skin removed
2 tablespoons snipped fresh chives
2 tablespoons lime juice
2 tablespoons extra-virgin olive oil,
extra
salt and cracked black pepper
1/3 cup crème fraîche
13/4 oz salmon roe

Toast both sides of the bread until
golden, then rub 1 side of each slice
with the halved garlic cloves and brush
generously with olive oil.
Cut the salmon fillets into 1/2-inch
dice, place in a nonmetallic bowl with
the chives, lime juice and olive oil
and season with salt and cracked
black pepper.
Serve the salmon tartare immediately
on the slices of bruschetta, topped
with a small spoonful each of crème
fraîche and salmon roe.

Serves 6

Dashi granules, made from dried tuna flakes and seaweed, are used in Japanese cooking to make stock.

# shrimp in blankets with a tokyo dipping sauce

Cut the wonton wrappers in half on the diagonal. Take 1 of these triangles and wrap half of it around the center of a shrimp. Brush the end with water and press firmly to seal. Wrap the remaining shrimp in the same manner.
Heat the oil in a wok to 350°F, or until a cube of bread browns in 15 seconds when added to the oil.
Cook the shrimp in batches for 2–3 minutes or until crisp, golden and cooked through.
To make the dipping sauce, place the dashi, water, shoyu and mirin in a bowl and whisk to combine.
Serve shrimp immediately with the dipping sauce.

Serves 4

9 oz package wonton wrappers
2 lb shrimp, peeled and deveined, tails left intact
oil, for deep-frying

*Tokyo dipping sauce*
1/4 teaspoon dashi granules
1/2 cup hot water
2 tablespoons shoyu (japanese soy sauce)
2 tablespoons mirin (sweet rice wine)

Verjuice is a sour liquid made from unripe grapes. If unavailable, use white wine vinegar instead.

## scallops with warm butter and shallot dressing

16 scallops
3 shallots, finely chopped
1/2 cup verjuice
1/3 cup butter, chilled and cut into 1/2 inch cubes
1 plum tomato, finely chopped
2 scallions, green part only, thinly sliced
salt and pepper
2 tablespoons extra-virgin olive oil

Place the shallots and verjuice in a small saucepan and bring to a boil. Cook for 2 minutes or until reduced by a third. Remove from the heat and whisk in the butter, a cube at a time. Stir in the tomato and scallions and season generously with salt and pepper. Set aside.

Heat the olive oil in a frying pan and cook the scallops in batches over high heat for 1 minute on each side. Arrange the scallops on small plates and drizzle over the warm butter dressing.

Serves 4

Scampi, or Dublin Bay prawns, look similar to large shrimp but have thicker shells and longer claws.

# barbecued scampi bathed in honey vinaigrette

Heat a lightly greased grill rack until hot and cook the scampi over a high heat until they are pink and tender. Place the garlic, mustard, honey, vinegar, lime juice and olive oil in a saucepan, add the butter and heat until boiling. Stir in the dill and pour the dressing over the scampi. Serve immediately with crusty bread.

Serves 4–6

20 scampi, or very large shrimp,
   heads removed and
   tails cut in half
3 cloves garlic, crushed
2 tablespoons whole grain mustard
3 tablespoons honey
1 tablespoon balsamic vinegar
3 tablespoons lime juice
1/2 cup light olive oil
2 tablespoons butter
2 tablespoons chopped fresh dill
crusty bread, to serve

# chu chee shrimp and scallops

*Chu Chee paste*
10 large dried red chiles
1 teaspoon coriander seeds
1 tablespoon white peppercorns
1 tablespoon shrimp paste
10 kaffir or young lime leaves, finely shredded
2 teaspoons grated lime zest
1 tablespoon chopped fresh cilantro stem and root
1 lemongrass stalk, white part only, finely chopped
3 tablespoons chopped fresh ginger or galangal
6 cloves garlic, chopped
10 red asian shallots or 3 medium spanish red onions, chopped

2 cups coconut cream (do not shake the can)
1 lb large shrimp, peeled and deveined
1 lb scallops
2–3 tablespoons fish sauce
3 tablespoons grated palm sugar or brown sugar
8 kaffir lime or young lime leaves, finely shredded
1 cup thai basil, or sweet basil, leaves

Preheat the oven to 350°F. Soak the chiles in a small bowl of hot water for 10 minutes. Drain, remove the seeds and roughly chop.

Place the coriander seeds, peppercorns and shrimp paste onto a foil-lined baking sheet and bake for 5 minutes or until fragrant.

Place these ingredients, plus all the remaining chu chee paste ingredients, into a food processor and process until the mixture forms a smooth paste. Add a little water if the paste is too stiff.

Spoon 1 cup of the thick coconut cream from the top of the can into a wok and heat until boiling. Stir in 5 tablespoons of the chu chee paste, reduce the heat and simmer for 10 minutes or until the oil begins to separate. Stir in the remaining coconut cream, shrimp and scallops and cook for 5 minutes. Add the fish sauce, palm sugar and lime leaves and cook for 3 minutes. Stir in half the basil and garnish with the remaining leaves.

Serves 4

# oysters three ways

Serve up this mixed platter of oysters.

To make bloody mary shots, place 6 oysters in 6 shot glasses, divide the vodka between the glasses, top with tomato juice, place a celery stalk into each one and season with tabasco, worcestershire and salt and pepper.
Makes 6

Place the soy sauce, sesame oil, mirin and sugar in a small saucepan and heat until the sugar dissolves. Slice the cucumber into fine ribbons and place in the bottom of the shell. Top with an oyster, drizzle with the sauce and sprinkle with ginger and sesame seeds.
Makes 12

Broil the prosciutto until crisp and allow to cool slightly before breaking into bite-sized pieces. To make the salsa, combine the tomato, bell peppers, onion, cilantro leaves and balsamic vinegar in a bowl. Serve some salsa and prosciutto pieces on each oyster, then top with a dollop of crème fraîche.
Makes 12

2 1/2 dozen fresh oysters

*Bloody mary shot*
3 tablespoons vodka
1/2 cup tomato juice
1 celery stalk, cut into small sticks
dash of tabasco sauce
dash of worcestershire sauce
salt and pepper

*Cucumber, ginger and sesame*
1/4 cup Japanese soy sauce
1 teaspoon sesame oil
1 tablespoon mirin (sweet rice wine)
1 teaspoon sugar
1 cucumber
2 tablespoons pickled ginger
2 tablespoons toasted sesame seeds

*Prosciutto and balsamic vinegar salsa*
4 slices prosciutto
1 plum tomato, finely diced
1/2 red bell pepper, diced
1/2 yellow bell pepper, diced
1 small red onion, finely chopped
1 tablespoon chopped fresh
   cilantro leaves
2 tablespoons balsamic vinegar
2 tablespoons crème fraîche

Used widely in Thai cooking,
garlic, pepper and cilantro root
make a wonderful combination.

# garlic pepper shrimp with green chile dip

2 tablespoons peanut oil
4 tablespoons chopped cilantro
root and stem
4 cloves garlic, roughly chopped
1 tablespoon white peppercorns
2 tablespoons palm sugar
2 tablespoons fish sauce
24 large shrimp

*Green chile dip*
2 tablespoons chopped cilantro
root and stem
2 cloves garlic, finely chopped
2 green chiles, finely chopped
4 tablespoons lime juice
2 tablespoons grated palm sugar
or brown sugar
2 tablespoons fish sauce

Place the oil, cilantro, garlic, white peppercorns, palm sugar and fish sauce into a food processor or mortar and pestle and process or pound to form a paste. Place the shrimp in a shallow, nonmetallic dish, add the paste and toss to coat. Cover and refrigerate for 3 hours.
Place all the dip ingredients in a bowl and stir to dissolve the sugar.
Once the shrimp have marinated, preheat a barbecue to high and cook the shrimp until they are pink and tender. Serve immediately with the dipping sauce.

Serves 4

Saffron—the orange stigma of the crocus flower—is the world's most expensive spice.

# mussels with saffron, lemongrass and tomatoes

Scrub the mussels and remove the hairy beards. Discard any that have opened or have broken shells. Heat the oil in a large saucepan and fry the onion, shallots and lemongrass until golden. Add the saffron and tomatoes and cook for 5 minutes or until the tomatoes start to soften. Add the wine and water and bring to a boil. Boil, covered, for 15 minutes. Add the mussels to the saucepan and cook, covered, for 5 minutes, shaking the saucepan occasionally until the mussels have opened. Discard any mussels that do not open. Stir in the garlic, sugar and parsley, and season with salt and cracked black pepper. Serve immediately with crusty bread.

Serves 4

3 lb black mussels
2 tablespoons olive oil
1 onion, finely chopped
6 shallots, finely chopped
2 lemongrass stalks, white part only, finely chopped
pinch saffron threads
6 plum tomatoes, chopped
1 cup dry white wine
1/2 cup water
2 cloves garlic, crushed
2 teaspoons sugar
2 tablespoons chopped fresh flat-leaf parsley
salt and cracked black pepper
crusty bread, to serve

To clean squid, gently pull the
tentacles down to remove the
insides, then peel away the skin.

## baby squid with caper flowers

2 lb baby squid
1 cup all-purpose flour
2 cloves garlic, crushed
pinch cayenne pepper
sea salt and pepper
oil, for deep-frying
2 tablespoons baby capers
in brine, well rinsed
1 cup chopped fresh flat-leaf parsley
lemon wedges, to serve

Clean the squid and cut the bodies into
1/2-inch thick rings. Pat dry with
paper towels.
Place the flour, garlic, cayenne pepper
and salt and pepper in a bowl and mix
to combine. Toss the squid in the flour
mixture in batches, shaking well to
remove any excess flour.
Heat the oil in a large saucepan until a
cube of bread browns in 15 seconds
when added to the saucepan. Deep-fry
the squid in batches for 2 minutes or
until crisp and golden. Sprinkle with
extra sea salt and drain on paper towels.
Deep-fry the capers for 30 seconds
or until they open out into "flowers".
Place the capers, squid and parsley in
a bowl and toss to combine. Sprinkle
with a little more sea salt and serve
with wedges of lemon.

Serves 4

There are about 250 varieties of snapper. Red snapper is highly regarded for its firm, sweet flesh.

# snapper pies

Preheat the oven to 425°F. Heat the oil in a deep frying pan, add the onions and stir over medium heat for 20 minutes or until the onions are slightly caramelized. Add the fish stock, bring to a boil and cook for 10 minutes or until the liquid is nearly evaporated. Stir in the cream and bring to a boil. Reduce the heat and simmer for 20 minutes, or until the liquid is reduced by half. Divide half the sauce among 4 2-cup ramekins. Place some fish pieces in each ramekin and top with the remaining sauce. Cut the pastry sheets slightly larger than the tops of the ramekins. Brush the edges of the pastry with a little of the egg, press the pastry onto the ramekins and brush the pastry top with the remaining beaten egg. Bake for 30 minutes, or until well puffed.

Serves 4

2 tablespoons olive oil
4 onions, thinly sliced
1 1/2 cups fish stock or broth
3 1/2 cups whipping cream
2 lb snapper fillets, skin removed, cut into large pieces
2 sheets frozen puff pastry, thawed
1 egg, lightly beaten

An octopus survives on a diet of clams and scallops. These contribute to its sweet flavor.

# char-grilled baby octopus

4 lb baby octopus, cleaned
1 1/2 cups red wine
3 tablespoons balsamic vinegar
2 tablespoons soy sauce
1/2 cup sweet chili sauce
1 cup thai basil, or sweet basil, leaves, to serve

Place the octopus, red wine and balsamic vinegar in a large, nonaluminum saucepan and bring to a boil. Reduce the heat and simmer for 15 minutes or until just tender. Drain and transfer to a bowl. Add the soy sauce and sweet chili sauce.
Heat a barbecue char-grill to high and cook the octopus until it is sticky and slightly charred. Serve on a bed of basil leaves.

Serves 4

# seafood risotto

Scrub the mussels and remove any that have opened. Place them in a saucepan with the white wine. Cover and cook over medium heat for 5 minutes or until the mussels open. Remove the meat from the shells and set aside. Discard any unopened mussels. Add the fish stock and saffron to the liquid that the mussels cooked in; slowly simmer.

Heat the oil and butter in a saucepan, add the onions, leek and lime zest and cook over medium heat for 5 minutes or until golden. Add the rice and stir for 1 minute or until translucent. Gradually add the stock to the rice, a cup at a time, stirring constantly until all the liquid has been absorbed and the risotto is creamy. Stir in half the mussels, scallops, shrimp and squid and cook for 5 minutes or until tender. Heat the butter in a frying pan, add the garlic and the remaining seafood in batches and cook over a high heat until golden brown. Stir the dill into the risotto. Place the risotto in bowls and top with the seafood.

Serves 4

10 oz mussels
3/4 cup dry white wine
3 cups fish stock or broth
pinch saffron threads
2 tablespoons olive oil
2 tablespoons butter
1 onion, finely chopped
1 leek, sliced
2 teaspoons grated lime zest
1 cup risotto arborio rice
10 oz scallops
1 lb shrimp, peeled and deveined
6 1/2 oz baby squid, cleaned
    and cut into rings
1/4 cup butter, extra
3 cloves garlic, finely chopped
1 tablespoon chopped fresh dill

Gravlax is a Swedish recipe
for curing fresh salmon.
It takes two days to prepare.

## gravlax with parmesan sheets

1 whole salmon, bones removed
1 bunch dill, finely chopped
3/4 cup sea salt or regular salt
1/4 cup sugar
1 tablespoon white peppercorns,
finely crushed
2 cups parmesan cheese,
finely grated
sour cream, to serve
cracked black pepper, to serve
chervil, to garnish

Place 1 salmon fillet skin side down in a large, shallow, nonmetallic dish. Combine the dill, salt, sugar and crushed peppercorns and spread this mixture over the length of the fillet. Place the second salmon fillet on top. Cover with plastic wrap and weigh down with a cutting board and some heavy cans. Refrigerate for 2 days, turning the salmon over as a whole piece every 12 hours and pouring off any excess liquid. When marinated, cut the salmon into wafer-thin slices.

To make the parmesan sheets, preheat the oven to 350°F. Thinly sprinkle the parmesan in triangle shapes onto 2 nonstick baking sheets lined with waxed paper. Bake for 10 minutes or until crisp. Top with gravlax, sour cream and black pepper. Garnish with chervil.

Serves 10–12

French green lentils have a deeper flavor than regular green lentils.

# herb-crusted tuna steaks with French green lentils and feta

Preheat the oven to 425°F. Heat the butter, oil, lime zest and garlic in a saucepan until the butter is melted. Add the herbs and remove from heat. Place the tuna steaks on a shallow, nonstick baking sheet and pour the butter mixture over them. Cut a small, deep cross in the top of each tomato, open out gently and stuff with feta. Place the tomatoes on a separate baking sheet to the fish and sprinkle both with salt and pepper. Bake the tomatoes for 20 minutes or until soft, and bake the fish for 10–15 minutes or until tender. Boil the lentils and bay leaf together in a saucepan with enough water to cover them. When tender, drain and toss with the lemon juice, extra olive oil and any juices from the baked tuna. Serve topped with tuna and tomato.

Serves 4

1 tablespoon butter
2 tablespoons extra-virgin olive oil
1 teaspoon grated lime zest
2 cloves garlic, crushed
3 tablespoons chopped mixed fresh herb leaves (sage, oregano, basil, parsley)
4 tuna steaks, any blood removed
8 small, vine-ripened tomatoes
3 1/2 oz marinated feta
sea salt and cracked black pepper
1 cup French green lentils
1 bay leaf
1 tablespoon lemon juice
1 tablespoon extra-virgin olive oil, extra

The French call scallops *coquilles Saint Jacques* after the patron saint of shellfish and shellfish gatherers.

# summer seafood marinara

10 oz fresh saffron or regular angel hair pasta
1 tablespoon extra-virgin olive oil
2 tablespoons butter
2 cloves garlic, finely chopped
1 large onion, finely chopped
1 small red chile, finely chopped
2 1/3 cups tomatoes, canned, peeled and chopped
1 cup white wine
zest of 1 lemon, grated
1/2 tablespoon sugar
6 1/2 oz scallops
1 lb shrimp, peeled and deveined
10 oz clams
salt and pepper

Cook the pasta in a large saucepan of rapidly boiling water until al dente. Drain and keep warm.

Heat the oil and butter in a large frying pan, add the garlic, onion and chile and cook over medium heat for 5 minutes or until soft but not golden. Add the tomatoes and wine and bring to a boil. Cook for 10 minutes or until the sauce has reduced and thickened slightly. Add the lemon zest, sugar, scallops, shrimp and clams and cook, covered, for 5 minutes or until the seafood is tender. Discard any shells that do not open. Season with salt and pepper. Serve the sauce on top of the pasta.

Serves 4

Make sure potatoes and fish are dry before plunging them into the hot oil, to prevent spitting.

# beer-battered fish with chunky fries

Sift the flour into a bowl and season generously with salt and pepper. Whisk in the beer to form a smooth batter. Heat the oil in a deep saucepan to 350°F, or until a cube of bread browns in 15 seconds when added to the oil. Cook the potatoes in batches until they are lightly golden. Drain on crumpled paper towels. Return the potatoes to the oil and cook until they are crisp and golden. Sprinkle with sea salt and keep warm.

Pat the fish fillets dry with paper towels. Coat the fish in the prepared batter and cook in batches in the hot oil for 3–5 minutes, depending on the size and thickness of the fish.

To make the tartar sauce, place all the tartar ingredients in a bowl and mix to combine. Serve with the fish.

Serves 4

1 cup all-purpose flour
sea salt or regular salt and pepper
1 cup chilled beer
oil, for deep-frying
2 lb large baking potatoes, peeled and cut into thick wedges
4 or 8 dogfish or other white-fleshed fillets (depending on their size)

*Tartar sauce*
3/4 cup whole egg mayonnaise
1/4 cup sour cream
6 gherkins, chopped
2 tablespoons capers
2 tablespoons chopped fresh parsley

Salted black beans—also known as Chinese black beans and fermented soy beans—are preserved in brine.

# black bean crab

8 blue crabs, cleaned and cut into halves or quarters, or 16 crab claws
1/3 cup peanut oil
4 cloves garlic, chopped
2 tablespoons grated fresh ginger
2 onions, finely chopped
51/2 oz salted black beans, rinsed and drained
1/3 cup fish stock or broth
2 tablespoons oyster sauce
2 teaspoons fish sauce
2 tablespoons soy sauce
3 tablespoons black bean sauce
1 tablespoon superfine sugar

Heat the oil in a wok until smoking, then cook the crab in batches until red and tender, adding more oil with each batch if needed. Remove the crab from the wok and drain off all but 2 tablespoons of oil.

Add the garlic, ginger and onions to the wok and cook over medium heat until golden. Stir in the black beans, fish stock, oyster sauce, fish sauce, soy sauce, black bean sauce and sugar and bring to a boil.

Add the crabs to the pan and simmer for 5–10 minutes or until heated through.

Serves 4

# individual caesars with sardines

To make the dressing, place the egg into a food processor, add the garlic, lemon juice, worcestershire sauce and anchovies and process to combine. With the motor running, add the oil in a thin, steady stream until the dressing is thickened slightly. Set aside. Place the bread crumbs, the grated parmesan and the parsley in a bowl and mix to combine. Place the beaten eggs and milk in another bowl and whisk to combine.

Dip the sardines into the egg mixture, then into the crumb mixture, and place on a waxed paper-lined baking sheet. Refrigerate for 1 hour. Heat the oil in a deep frying pan until hot, or until a cube of bread browns in 15 seconds when added to the pan. Deep-fry the pappadams until crisp, and set aside on paper towels. Deep-fry the sardines in batches until crisp and golden brown. Arrange lettuce leaves on a plate, top with prosciutto, sardines, papads and parmesan drizzled with dressing.

Serves 4

*Dressing*

1 egg
2 cloves garlic
2 tablespoons lemon juice
1/2 teaspoon worcestershire sauce
3–4 anchovy fillets
1/2 cup extra-virgin olive oil

1 cup dry bread crumbs
2/3 cup grated parmesan cheese
2 tablespoons chopped fresh parsley
2 eggs, lightly beaten
1/3 cup milk
16 butterflied sardines
oil, for deep-frying
12 baby papads, cooked and broken into pieces
1 baby romaine lettuce, leaves separated
8 prosciutto slices, broiled until crisp
1/2 cup parmesan cheese, shaved

Octopus and squid are cephalods—which means "headfooted." Their tentacles sprout from their heads.

# barbecued sweet chili seafood on banana mats

1 lb shrimp, peeled and deveined, tails left intact
10 oz scallops
1 lb baby squid, cleaned and bodies cut in quarters
1 lb baby octopus, cleaned
1 cup sweet chili sauce
1 tablespoon fish sauce
2 tablespoons lime juice
3 tablespoons peanut oil
banana leaves, cut into squares, to serve
lime wedges, to serve

Place the shrimp, scallops, squid and octopus in a shallow, nonmetallic bowl. In a separate bowl combine the sweet chili sauce, fish sauce, lime juice and 1 tablespoon of the peanut oil. Pour the mixture over the seafood and mix gently to coat. Allow to marinate for 1 hour. Drain the seafood well and reserve the marinade. Heat the remaining oil on a greased grill rack. Cook the seafood in batches (depending on the size of your barbecue) over high heat for 3–5 minutes or until tender. Drizzle each batch with a little of the leftover marinade during cooking. Pile the seafood high onto the squares of banana leaf and serve with wedges of lime, if desired.

Serves 4

Black peppercorns are the berries
of the Indian peppercorn plant. The
berries are picked unripe, then dried.

# rare pepper-crusted tuna with lemon hollandaise sauce

To make the hollandaise sauce, place the egg yolks, mustard, lemon zest and lemon juice in a food processor and, with the motor running, add the melted butter in a thin, steady stream. Chill until ready to serve. Place the peppercorns in a mortar and pestle and pound until roughly cracked. Remove any blood from the tuna fillet, then cut the fillet into thick batons approximately 2 inches wide x 3/4 inch thick. Coat the tuna on all sides with the pepper. Heat the oil in a large, nonstick frying pan, cook the tuna fillets for 30 seconds on each side, then remove from the frying pan and allow to rest for 5 minutes. Cut the lemon in half and squeeze the juice over the tuna. Cut the tuna into 1/2-inch thick slices and serve with the lemon hollandaise sauce.

Serves 4

*Lemon hollandaise sauce*
2 egg yolks
2 teaspoons dijon mustard
1 teaspoon finely grated lemon zest
1–2 tablespoons lemon juice
1/2 cup butter, melted

1/3 cup black peppercorns
1 1/2 lb tuna fillet
oil, for frying
1 lemon

Swordfish take their name from the sword-like projection that extends from their upper jaw.

## swordfish stacks with salsa verde

*Salsa verde*
1 cup flat-leaf parsley leaves, finely chopped
1 tablespoon gherkins, finely chopped
2 tablespoons baby capers
1 tablespoon anchovies, chopped
4 cloves garlic, finely chopped
3 tablespoons red wine vinegar
1/3 cup extra-virgin olive oil

1 large eggplant, cut into 1/2-inch thick slices
1/4 cup extra-virgin olive oil
4 swordfish steaks
2 tablespoons balsamic vinegar
4 vine-ripened tomatoes
61/2 oz bocconcini (baby mozzarella)
1/2 cup whole basil leaves

Make the salsa verde by combining the parsley, gherkins, capers, anchovies and garlic in a bowl, then whisking in the red wine vinegar and olive oil. Set aside. Brush the eggplant slices with olive oil and cook under a hot broiler until golden brown on both sides. Drain on paper towels.

Cut the swordfish steaks into 3 pieces on the diagonal. Heat a little more oil in a large frying pan and cook the swordfish over high heat until golden brown and cooked through. Leave the fish in the pan and add the balsamic vinegar. Cook until sticky. Cut the tomatoes and bocconcini into thick slices. Layer the eggplant, basil, tomato, bocconcini and swordfish and drizzle over the salsa verde dressing.

Serves 4

Place live crabs in the freezer
several hours prior to cooking
them. This puts them to sleep.

# chile crab

Use a cleaver to cut each crab into quarters, then crack the claws with the back of the cleaver. Heat the oil in a wok until hot, or until a cube of bread browns in 15 seconds when added to the pan. Fry the crab pieces in batches until they turn crisp or red on each side.
Drain off half the oil and discard. Reheat the remaining oil and cook the garlic, ginger, onions and chiles over medium heat for 3 minutes. Stir in the sauces and sugar and bring to a boil. Return the crabs to the wok and cook for 10 minutes. Finally, season with the tamarind concentrate and soy sauce and garnish with cilantro leaves. Serve immediately with steamed rice.

Serves 4–6

2 Dungeness crabs, cleaned and cut
    into quarters, or 16–20 crab claws
1/2 cup peanut oil
4 cloves garlic, finely chopped
1 tablespoon grated fresh ginger
2 onions, finely chopped
4 small red chiles, seeded and
    finely chopped
1/2 cup tomato ketchup
1/2 cup bottled asian chili sauce
2 tablespoons sugar
1 tablespoon tamarind concentrate
1 tablespoon soy sauce
fresh cilantro leaves, to garnish
steamed rice, to serve

To prevent spitting of oil, make sure the fish is absolutely dry before you add it to the wok.

# whole lemongrass fish with sticky chili sauce

1 lemongrass stalk, cut in half and into 2-inch lengths
1 large red snapper, 1 lb 10 oz, slit in 3 places at its thickest part
oil, for deep-frying
5 red asian shallots or 2 small red spanish onions, sliced
4 cloves garlic, sliced
2 tablespoons vegetable oil, extra
2 bird's-eye (Thai) chiles, thinly sliced
1/2 cup grated palm sugar or brown sugar
4 tablespoons fish sauce
4 tablespoons tamarind concentrate
4 tablespoons lime juice
fresh cilantro leaves, to garnish

Place lemongrass pieces into the incisions in the snapper. Heat the deep-frying oil in a wok until hot, or until a cube of bread browns in 15 seconds when added to it. Deep-fry the fish until one side is crisp and golden. Turn and cook the other side. Remove and drain on paper towels. Add the shallots and garlic to the wok and cook until golden. Remove. Do not overcook the shallots or garlic or they will be bitter.

Heat the extra vegetable oil in a saucepan, add the chiles, palm sugar, fish sauce, tamarind concentrate and lime juice and stir until the sugar dissolves. Bring to a boil and cook until the sauce is syrupy. Pour the syrup over the crisp fish and serve immediately, garnished with the cilantro leaves, shallots and garlic.

Serves 4

Sea salt flakes are made by evaporating salt water using either the heat of the sun or fire.

# salt and pepper squid

Pat the squid bodies dry. Place them on a cutting board with the soft insides facing up, and use a sharp knife to make a fine diamond pattern, taking care not to cut all the way through. Cut the bodies into small rectangles and place them in a bowl. Cover with milk and lemon juice and refrigerate for 15 minutes. Place the salt, peppercorns and sugar in a mortar and pestle or spice grinder and pound or process to a fine powder. Transfer to a bowl and stir in the cornstarch. Dip the squid into the egg white, then toss to coat in the salt-and-pepper mixture, shaking off any excess. Heat the oil in a large frying pan or wok to 350°F, or until a cube of bread browns in 15 seconds. Cook the squid in batches until crisp and lightly golden. Serve with lime wedges.

Serves 4 as an entrée

2 lb baby squid, cleaned and bodies cut in half
1 cup milk
2 tablespoons lemon juice
2 tablespoons sea salt
1 1/2 tablespoons white peppercorns
2 teaspoons sugar
2 cups cornstarch
4 egg whites, lightly beaten
oil, for deep-frying
lime wedges, to serve

Jasmine rice, or Thai fragrant rice, is a delicately scented long-grain rice. The grains stay loose when cooked.

## poached halibut with jasmine papaya salad

1/3 cup jasmine rice
3 cloves garlic
2 small red chiles, finely chopped
1/4 cup dried shrimp
2 cups finely shredded green papaya
8 cherry tomatoes, quartered
2 tablespoons lime juice
2 tablespoons fish sauce
1 tablespoon grated light palm or brown sugar
1 2/3 cups coconut milk
1 cup fish stock
4 kaffir lime or young lime leaves, finely shredded
2 lemongrass stalks, halved lengthwise
1 tablespoon grated fresh ginger
4 halibut fillets, cut in half through the center

Follow the manufacturer's instructions to cook the rice. Place the garlic, chiles and dried shrimp in a mortar and pestle and pound until combined. Transfer to a nonmetallic bowl and stir in the cooked rice, papaya and tomatoes.

Place the lime juice, fish sauce and palm sugar in a bowl and whisk to combine. Pour the dressing over the salad and toss to combine.

Place the coconut milk, fish stock, lime leaves, lemongrass and ginger in a large frying pan and heat until simmering. Add the fish and cook for 5 minutes or until tender. Remove the fish and boil the coconut milk until slightly thickened. Serve 2 halibut fillets stacked on top of each other with the sauce spooned over. Accompany with green papaya salad.

Serves 4

Tagine is a Moroccan-style stew simmered with vegetables and flavored with spices.

# moroccan seafood tagine

Preheat oven to 350°F. Cut the fish into large cubes. Peel and devein the shrimp; leave the tails intact. Heat the oil in a large casserole, add the onions and spices and cook over medium heat for 5 minutes or until the onions are soft and the spices are fragrant. Add the vegetables and 2 cups of water and bake, covered, in the oven, for 40 minutes. Remove the top, add the seafood, prunes, honey and preserved lemon and bake, uncovered, for another 10 minutes.

Place the couscous in a bowl with the butter and orange blossom water and cover with boiling water. Allow to rest for 10 minutes, or until all the liquid has been absorbed. Serve the couscous in a ring with the tagine in the center. Sprinkle with almonds.

Serves 4

1 lb goatfish or ocean perch fillets
1 lb shrimp
2 tablespoons vegetable oil
1 large onion, chopped
1 teaspoon ground ginger
pinch saffron threads
2 teaspoons ground coriander
2 teaspoons ground cumin
1/2 teaspoon chili powder
1 teaspoon ground cinnamon
10 oz sweet potatoes, cut into chunks
3/4 lb potatoes, cut into chunks
2 tomatoes, chopped
2 zucchini, cut into thick slices
1 cup prunes
1 tablespoon honey
1 tablespoon sliced preserved lemon
12/3 cups couscous
2 tablespoons butter
1 teaspoon orange flower water
2 tablespoons toasted slivered almonds

*Zuppa di pesce* is Italian for fish soup. Use whatever fresh seafood you have available.

## zuppa di pesce

1 lb squid
1 lb clams
1 lb shrimp, peeled and deveined, tails left intact
1 lb goatfish or ocean perch fillets
3 tablespoons extra-virgin olive oil
1 onion, finely chopped
1 red chile, finely chopped
3 cloves garlic, finely chopped
1 cup dry white wine
2 bay leaves
4 large vine-ripened tomatoes, peeled, seeded and chopped
3 cups fish stock or broth
pinch saffron threads
salt and pepper
crusty Italian bread, to serve

Clean all the seafood and cut the fish fillets into bite-sized pieces.

Heat the oil in a large saucepan, add the onion, chile and garlic and cook over low heat for 10 minutes, or until the onion is soft and golden (do not allow the onion to brown). Add the wine and bring to a boil, cooking over high heat until reduced by half. Reduce the heat, add the bay leaves, tomatoes and stock and simmer for 5 minutes. Add the seafood. Cover and cook for 5 minutes or until the seafood is tender. Discard any clam shells that do not open. Stir in the saffron and season with salt and pepper. Serve with bread.

Serves 4–6

Cannellini beans are creamy white beans widely used in Italian cooking. If short on time, use canned beans.

## summer crab and bean salad

Soak the cannellini beans in cold water overnight. Drain, place the beans in a large saucepan, cover with water and bring to a boil. Reduce the heat and simmer for 20 minutes. Drain and allow the cooked beans to cool slightly. Cook the pepper skin side up under a hot broiler until the skin blackens and blisters. Place in a plastic bag and allow to cool, then peel away the skin. Cut into strips and add to the beans. Stir in the garlic, parsley, lemon juice, olive oil, crab meat and red onion and refrigerate for 2 hours. Season generously with salt and cracked black pepper. Serve with crusty bread.

Serves 4–6

3/4 cup dried cannellini beans
1 red bell pepper, cut into large pieces
3 cloves garlic, finely chopped
1/2 cup fresh flat-leaf parsley, chopped
1/2 cup lemon juice
1/4 cup extra-virgin olive oil
10 oz fresh or canned crab meat
1 red onion, thinly sliced
salt and cracked black pepper
crusty bread, to serve

# lobster kiev

1/2 cup butter, softened
2 cloves garlic, crushed
1 teaspoon lemon zest, grated
1 tablespoon chopped fresh chives
1 tablespoon chopped fresh chervil
1 tablespoon chopped fresh parsley
4 large uncooked lobster tails
1 cup all-purpose flour
salt and pepper
1 egg, lightly beaten
2 cups fresh white bread crumbs
oil, to deep-fry
steamed fresh asparagus spears, to serve

Preheat the oven to 350°F. Combine the butter, garlic, zest and herbs in a bowl. Spoon this mixture onto a sheet of plastic wrap and roll into a log shape. Freeze until firm.

Remove the lobster meat from the shell by using scissors to cut down both sides of the shell on the underside. Peel back the soft undershell and gently pull out the flesh in one piece. Remove the black vein. Make a deep pocket down the length of each tail, taking care not to cut all the way through. Slice up the butter and place two or three disks into each pocket. Dip the tails in flour that has been seasoned with salt and pepper, then dip them in egg and then bread crumbs. Refrigerate for 30 minutes. Deep-fry the tails in batches in hot oil for 5 minutes or until crisp and golden. Transfer to a baking sheet and bake for 5 minutes, or until cooked through. Serve sliced on top of steamed asparagus.

Serves 4

# salmon burgers with tzatziki

To make the tzatziki, place the cucumber, mint, garlic and yogurt in a bowl and mix well. Set aside.

To make the patties, first place the bread in a food processor and process into crumbs. Finely chop the salmon to resemble ground meat. (Do not do this in the food processor—the fish will get pasty.) Place the salmon, bread crumbs, scallions, lemon juice, dill, cumin and egg in a bowl. Mix well. Divide the mixture into 4 and shape each piece into patties. Cover and refrigerate for 1 hour.

Heat half the oil in a frying pan, add the fennel bulbs and cook until golden brown and slightly caramelized. Cut the bread into 4 and then in half through the center. Toast if you prefer a crisp sandwich. Heat the remaining oil in a nonstick frying pan and cook the patties over medium heat for 3–5 minutes on each side. To serve, place a few leaves of your choice onto the bottom layer of bread and top the burger with tzatziki, fried fennel and tomatoes.

Serves 4

*Tzatziki*
1 cucumber, finely chopped
2 tablespoons chopped fresh mint
2 cloves garlic, crushed
1/3 cup natural, thick yogurt

2 slices white bread, crusts removed
1 lb 10 oz salmon fillets, skin and
  bones removed
2 scallions, finely chopped
1 tablespoon lemon juice
2 tablespoons chopped fresh dill
2 teaspoons ground cumin
1 egg, lightly beaten
4 tablespoons extra-virgin olive oil
3 baby fennel bulbs, sliced
1 turkish bread or focaccia loaf
lettuce leaves, to serve
2/3 cup sun-dried tomatoes, to serve

Throughout the Mediterranean it is possible to find a variety of pickled or preserved seafood.

# mediterranean pickled seafood salad

1/4 cup olive oil
1/2 cup white wine vinegar
2/3 cup dry white wine
3 cloves garlic, thinly sliced
1 lb black mussels, cleaned and debearded
2 lb baby octopus, cleaned
2 lb squid, cleaned and sliced
1 lb shrimp, peeled and deveined, tails left intact
zest of 1 lemon
zest of 1 orange
3/4 cup sun-dried tomatoes in oil
4 scallions, sliced
1 tablespoon thyme leaves
1 tablespoon basil leaves, shredded
1/4 cup lemon juice
crusty bread, to serve
lemon wedges, to serve

Place the olive oil, vinegar, white wine and garlic in a saucepan. Bring to a boil and simmer over low heat for 10 minutes. Add the mussels and cook for 5 minutes or until the shells open. Remove the mussels from the pan, discarding any that have not opened, and remove the meat from the shells, placing it into a large bowl. Add the octopus to the pickling liquid and cook for 40 minutes or until tender. Remove and add the squid and shrimp and cook for 5 minutes. Drain and discard the liquid. Add the zests, tomatoes (with their oil), scallions, thyme, basil and lemon juice to the seafood and mix to combine. Cover and refrigerate for 24–48 hours. Return to room temperature and serve with crusty bread and lemon wedges.

Serves 4

Known as tod man pla in Thailand, these fish patties are eaten as snacks with a sweet chili sauce.

# thai fish cakes with sweet chili sauce

Combine the cucumber, chiles, sugar, water, rice vinegar and cilantro in a bowl and mix well to dissolve the sugar. Set this dipping sauce aside. Place the fish, shrimp and curry paste in a food processor and process to form a smooth, sticky paste. Transfer to a bowl and, with your hands, mix in the beans, lime leaves and basil. Shape tablespoons of the mixture into small balls, then flatten them with the palm of your hand. Cover and refrigerate for 1 hour. Heat the oil in a wok until hot, or until a cube of bread browns in 15 seconds when added to the oil. Cook the fish cakes in batches for 2 minutes or until browned and cooked through. Drain on paper towels and serve with the cucumber dipping sauce.

Serves 4–6

*Cucumber dipping sauce*
1 cucumber, seeded and finely diced
2 small red chiles, finely chopped
4 tablespoons grated palm sugar, or brown sugar
1 tablespoon water
6 tablespoons rice vinegar
1 tablespoon chopped fresh cilantro leaves

1 lb redfish fillets, skin removed
6 1/2 oz shrimp, peeled and deveined
3 tablespoons thai red curry paste
1/2 cup yard-long or green beans, sliced
4 kaffir or young lime leaves, finely shredded
6 thai basil, or sweet basil, leaves, shredded
oil, for deep-frying

Skordalia is the Greek name for a dish of puréed potatoes flavored with garlic, olive oil and lemons.

# salmon on skordalia with saffron-lime butter

*Skordalia*
1 lb potatoes, peeled and diced
3 cloves garlic, finely chopped
juice of 1 lime
1/2 cup milk
1/2 cup virgin olive oil

*Saffron-lime butter*
1/3 cup butter
pinch saffron threads
2 tablespoons lime juice

4 salmon fillets, approximately 61/2 oz each
2 tablespoons oil, for frying
1 tablespoon lime zest, to garnish
chervil leaves, to garnish

To make the skordalia, cook the potatoes until soft, then drain and place into a food processor. Process the potatoes, garlic, lime juice, milk and olive oil until smooth and creamy.

To make the saffron-lime butter, melt the butter in a saucepan, add the saffron and lime juice and cook until the butter turns a nutty brown color.

Pat the salmon fillets dry. Heat the oil in a frying pan and cook the salmon, skin side down, over high heat for 2–3 minutes on each side, or until the skin is crisp and golden brown. Turn and cook the other side.

Serve the salmon on top of the skordalia with the saffron-lime butter spooned over the top. Garnish with lime zest and chervil leaves.

Serves 4

# teriyaki barbecued salmon

To make the broth, pour the liquid in which the mushrooms were soaked into a saucepan. Add the dashi granules, soy sauce, mirin and superfine sugar and bring to a boil. Simmer for 5 minutes.

Place the salmon, mushrooms, teriyaki marinade, honey and sesame oil into a nonmetallic dish and allow to marinate for 15 minutes.

Bring a large saucepan of water to a boil and cook the noodles for 3–4 minutes or until tender. Drain. Heat a lightly greased grill rack. Take the salmon and mushrooms out of the marinade and cook over high heat for 3 minutes on each side. (Do not overcook the salmon—it should be slightly rare in the center.) Pour the reserved marinade from the fish over during cooking.

To serve, divide the noodles among 4 serving bowls, pour over the broth from the mushrooms, then top with the salmon and mushrooms and sprinkle with the scallions.

Serves 4

12 dried chinese mushrooms, (e.g. shiitakes, cloud ear) rehydrated in 2 cups of boiling water
1 teaspoon dashi granules
1/4 cup japanese soy sauce
2 tablespoons mirin (sweet rice wine)
1/2 teaspoon superfine sugar
4 salmon cutlets, 5 oz each
1/4 cup teriyaki marinade
1 tablespoon honey
1 teaspoon sesame oil
8 oz dried soba noodles
2 scallions, sliced on the diagonal

Preserved grape leaves come in cans, packed in brine. If you have fresh leaves, simmer for 10 minutes.

# rainbow trout smoked in grape leaves

1 cup hickory smoking chips
1/2 cup dry white wine
4 rainbow trout
1 lemon, thinly sliced
4 sprigs oregano
8 grape leaves

*Preserved lemon butter*
1/2 cup butter
1 tablespoon chopped fresh oregano
1 tablespoon preserved lemon, pith and flesh removed, peel finely chopped
1 clove garlic, crushed

Preheat a covered barbecue until the charcoal turns white. Place the smoking chips and wine in a nonmetallic bowl and allow to rest for 15 minutes. Pat the trout dry using paper towels and place a few slices of lemon and a sprig of oregano into the cavity of each fish. Wrap two grape leaves around each trout and secure with kitchen string. Scatter the smoking chips over the hot coals. Place the trout on a lightly greased grill rack, cover and allow to smoke for 10 minutes or until tender. To make the preserved lemon butter, mix together the butter, oregano, lemon peel and garlic. Spread the butter on a lightly greased baking sheet to a 1/2–3/4-inch thickness and freeze until solid. Cut the butter into slices and serve on top of the hot smoked trout.

Serves 4

Published by Time-Life Books, a division of Time Life Inc.
Time-Life is a trademark of Time Warner Inc. and affiliated companies.

Time-Life Books
Vice President and Publisher: Neil S. Levin
Vice President, Content Development: Jennifer L. Pearce
Senior Sales Director: Richard J. Vreeland
Director, Marketing and Publicity: Inger Forland
Director of New Product Development: Carolyn M. Clark
Director of Custom Publishing: John Lalor
Director of Rights and Licensing: Olga Vezeris
Executive Editor: Linda Bellamy
Director of Design: Tina Taylor

First published in 2000 by Murdoch Books®,
a division of Murdoch Magazines Pty Ltd,
GPO Box 1203, Sydney, NSW Australia 2001

Photographer: Ben Dearnley
Stylist: Kristen Anderson
Concept & Design: Marylouise Brammer
Project Manager: Anna Waddington
Editor: Susan Gray
Recipe Testing: Valli Little, Angela Tregonning

Group General Manager: Mark Smith
Publisher: Kay Scarlett
Production Manager: Liz Fitzgerald

Library of Congress Cataloging-in-Publication Data available upon request.
ISBN 0-7370-3032-1

Printed by Toppan Printing Hong Kong Co. Ltd.
PRINTED IN CHINA. This edition printed 2001.